A collection of poems

Other books by Irfan Virk

My Mate's as 'Ard as Nails (My Obdurate Companion)
My Mate Could Talk for England (My Voluble Companion)
The BBC Micro:bit and the Moon Dust Aliens
The Fine Artist in Me

Soft Brass

A Collection of Poems

Irfan Virk

Daisy-i

Soft Brass
A collection of Poems

A CIP catalogue record for this book is available from the British Library.

ISBN: 978-1-9163290-4-1

Daisy-i Limited
Pera Business Park
Nottingham Road
Melton Mowbray
LE13 0PB

To the memory of my grandparents

Contents

Soft Brass Poems

Virk

Soft Brass

Soft brass rising above the hills and dales
On a morning enfolded in lamp black
Soft burbling brass rising unchallenged
Through cerulean blues and cirrus skies
A brassy cortège bearing a dead weight

Soft brass passing through lines of Prussian blues
Past the swirling wraiths lost in time and space
Past the demigods held in abeyance
Soft brass marking time, meeting the darkness
And heading out beyond the starry sky

Beyond the celestial horizon
Beyond the realm of starlight, awakened
By soft caressing brass, a mortal soul
Emerging into the void cognisant
Of the nature of immortality

Soft brass falling across the hills and dales
On a morning enveloped in sunlight
Sustained by the breath of a living well
Leaving behind an insistent echo
To guide a mortal soul to Heavens veil

The Parasitic President

He parades as a patriot
His true nature concealed
His breast is heavy laden
He would have you believe
Great deeds (he claims) are his legacy
In the service of his country
All else is fake news

Behind the flag, a parasite
His tax returns concealed
He is the truest of men
He would have you believe
Great have been his tax contributions
Swelling the lifeblood of the nation
All else is fake news

Have they? Is it?
His twitching tail
Gives the game away

His bloated buttocks are revealed
For doubters still, to see
Engorged and heavy laden (they are)
With the fruits of his sins
Great misdeeds are his legacy
In the service of his country
All else is fake news

Behind the feigned patriotism
A corrupter of souls
Pity the children of these
Innocents fed on lies
Great jeopardy will be their legacy
For the mortal souls of their progeny
All else is fake news

Time then to renew, time to say adieu
And render greatly to him
His just and righteous due

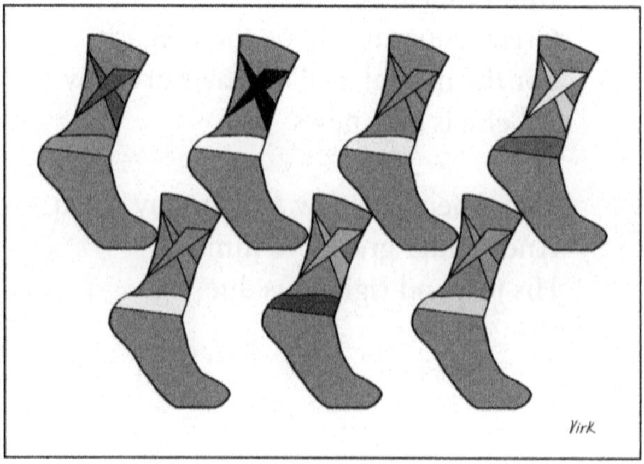
Virk

Socks

Picture yourself in a suit or a frock
Meandering down Piccadilly Docks
Incongruous ankles may easily shock
Unthinkable is a world without socks

Seven pairs of socks are all a man needs
To colour his whims and play fashion's lead
Imagine the colours of daring deed
Defining your ankles with lines of speed

In winter, spring, summer and autumn sun
Made glorious for occasions to run
An essential covering for everyone
Form and function enwrapped in cotton spun

The Sounds of Christmas

A frosty wind is blowing hard
Advent calendars stand on guard
The year will soon be at an end
The sounds of Christmas will attend

Children in the playground singing
Church bells in the distance ringing
Nativity plays mark the date
The sounds of Christmas lie in wait

Sleigh bells jingling over Northants
Wassailers shivering in hot pants
Shop tills kerchinging in the night
The sounds of Christmas taking flight

Uncles, nephews, nieces and aunts
Nan and grandad leading the chants
We're all singing God save the Queen
The sounds of Christmas so serene

But there is one sound that we don't mention
Indulging instead in misdirection
What could it be that's too late to rescind?
The sound, of course, of Santa breaking wind

Windmills

Two windmills in the distance, a glance apart
Blinking, blinking each in remorseless start
Flighty Barbarella white against blue
Pouring her heart out to the azure hue
Benjamin Leisurely white against green
Quietly burnishing his sails unseen
Out of kilter condemned forever each
To whisper sweet nothings to one out of reach

Starlings

The light is fast fading now, can you see
The blackberries whispering their secrets
To the starlings gathering in the hedgerows?
Unseen, the badgers slowly saunter past
Heading for the banks of soft sandy soil

The darkening leaves are being released
From the bewitchment of the setting sun
They fall to each other in soft embrace
Casually, nonchalantly, the badgers
Begin repairing their winter retreat

The starlings, drunk on the promises of
Mysteries launch themselves into the sky
Silhouetted in the silvery light
The badgers are ejecting the foxes
Interlopers residing in their sett

Hiding in the smallest of crevices
The curious mice are watching the scene
Whiskers quivering, eyes glistening, ears twitching
Wiping their paws in smug satisfaction
The clan start foraging for new bedding

Promenading up on high, the starlings
In harmonious and joyful temper
Sing to the blackberries in the hedgerows
The shy badgers, the foxes and the mice
Look to the sky and begin to applaud

Paused

Watching sparrows in my garden
Watching waves whilst begging pardon
Watching insects crossing my path
Watching a small boy gazing south

Watching vapour trails in the sky
Watching languid kites drifting by
Watching May becoming bolder
Watching pebbles growing older

Waiting for my beloved wife
I am paused in this sad half-life

Tadpoles

We first met when we were tiny tadpoles
Doting parents watched as we played our roles
She wore a cap and swim suit, blue and white
My red jammers must have seemed awfully bright

Our colours in the baby pool combined
To make, I thought, a union flag entwined
I know I fell in love right then and there
With a tadpole named Jennifer St Claire

As dolphins, we tumbled and turned anew
In our hearts as Olympians, we flew
Brest stroke, back stroke, front crawl and butterfly
With every passing stroke she made me sigh

Then came into our lives an odd teacher
One who described him herself as pure nature
who made us wonder about pudenda
And left us confused about our gender

I looked again at Jennifer St Claire
Wondering if I would still find her there
I'm told that I've become a hobbledehoy
But God please don't turn her into a boy

Redemption

When I was a young lad, I was a tartar
Nickin' mum's biscuits was just for starters
Soon I was stealin' from the corner shop
In those days it was just about lollipops
I never worried much about wooden tops

When I was thirteen, I left school and turned pro
Burglary and theft was such easy dough
While kids at school were lightin' up jam jars
Dad was teaching me how to break into cars
Pretty soon I was learnin' 'bout turf wars

Mum and dad taught us the family trade
Brothers and sisters, we all made the grade
When I robbed a bank, my dad threw a party
But in jail there's no time for fine malarkey
Time enough though, to listen to Satie

My mum died six months after I went inside
At her funeral we stood by her side
Me, my wife and my new born son and I
Pondered on redemption and corruption's eye
Cancerous and unblinking in the sky

Gazing upon our son we came to see
Enslavement of generations yet to be
And in that moment, we also came to see
That redemption lay in our son's liberty
And so, we resolved a foundling he would be

Virk

Sleaford Ducks

Sleepy Sleaford ducks
Sleeping by the river
Top and tail eyes keeping watch
On the kittens playing hopscotch
Wake up wake up
Wake up sleepy ducks

Chirping Sleaford ducklings
Chirping in the river
In the wake of their mother
In a line behind each other
Keep up keep up
Keep up little ducks

Quacking Sleaford ducks
Quacking by the river
In panic and disorder
Fleeing from a frightful toddler
Give up give up
Give up quacking ducks

Bubbly Sleaford ducks
Bubbling by the river
Being fed from a bread bin
By the statue of Bernie Taupin
Fill your cups fill your cups
Fill your cups, lucky Sleaford ducks

Animal Noises

Did you know that monkeys can talk?
Did you know that they can use verbs?
And pronouns and direct objects?
What are the odds they'll soon embark
On writing blank verse just for a lark

Oh! they already are, you say
So, what kind of stuff do they write?
They write about important stuff
Like rock and roll and good school places
Love and hate and three-legged races

Did you know that Dolphins can sing?
Did you know that they like rice pudding?
And digestives and Jaffa cakes?
What are the odds that they'll soon start
Bartering rides for cinnamon tarts

Oh! they already are you say
So, what kind of rides do they give?
They only give important rides
Like to the dentists and to the races
Hold tight and make sure to wear braces

Anyway

Adam and Allison, architects and
Aubrey and Abigail, aviators and
Adam's aunt Ada are asking about
Abseiling abroad anywhere at all

All awhile, assassins are arriving
And aliens are abducting A-listers,
Addled Americans and Austrians

Arthur and Arianne, accountants and
Aidan and Adeline, acrobats and
Arthur's aunt Aileen are advising about
Arresting art and afternoon affairs

All awhile, archangels are advancing
Angelic accoutrements adorning
And amongst acquaintances an affray

Alan and Aisha, arsonists and
Abel and Athena, agitators and
Alan's aunt Agnes affraying all about
Advanced assonance and alliteration

Anyway, August and April are ambling
Ambling, ambling along, amorously
Arming ambling, Ad astra ambulant

Donkey Tales

I dream of verdant fields and wild hedgerows
I dream of soft scents and the sound of bees
Far from the crowds and the smell of seaweed

They call me Pedro which is not my name
Even Bonnie thinks that's funny and she laughed
When Horace tipped salt water in my jug

I dream of living on a high hill top
Within touching distance of passing clouds
So quiet they would make for ideal neighbours

The other thing I don't like is the sand
Though she doesn't mean to, Doris always
Manages to kick the stuff in my face

I dream of watching slow trains passing by
Along a valley floor far, far below
They needn't be steam trains, diesels would do

Eli gave us our breakfast this morning
To give him his due, he tried to be fair
But Horace tricked him and he stole my share

I'm too hungry for day dreaming today
Today I can feel the weight on my back
And I'm starting to hear funny noises

Long past lights out I kick open the door
Footsteps running behind me down the lane
Bonnie and Doris both hot on my tail

Heading north-west by north seeking high ground
I can hear the sound of falling water
Ravens guide us in, the Clyde falls away

Virk

Sleaford Skies

Flute and horn concerto in C
Sunlight bouncing off vaporous seas
Kale and cabbages in the fields
The umbers of the earth revealed

Steel pylons dissecting the land
Migrant workers lending a hand
Gentle winds blowing towards the Rhine
White clouds processing in slow slow time

All the while a princess lies asleep
In Lincolnshire fields wide and deep
Royal lanterns mark her sleeping sighs
Glittering orbs above Sleaford skies

The Billy Buoy

We used to walk along this beach every day
To the Billy Buoy especially in May
Carrying bundles of joy in our arms
But they are gone now; all that remains are psalms

Our arms hang heavy as we walk every day
To the Billy Buoy especially in May
I try often to take her hand in mine
But she is lost to the horizon-line

Perhaps they will come again with their own
Bundles of joy enwrapped in gowns newly sewn
Until then we are left alone and must fain
To dwell on the aftertaste of love's refrain

Cuties

Brother and sister
Flying so high
Cousins in the fray
High up in the Milky Way
Everyone a cutie

Is that my Granddad?
Is that my Nan?
Aunts in the frame
They all remember my name
Everyone a cutie

Shamim come and see
He's hurt his knee
They're saying good-byes
Guess what I've got in my eyes
All such cuties

Printed in Great Britain
by Amazon

49125795R00020